BEST EVER
SMOOTHIES
& JUICES

A COLLECTION OF OVER **100** ESSENTIAL RECIPES

This edition published in 2011
LOVE FOOD is an imprint of Parragon Books Ltd

Parragon
Queen Street House
4 Queen Street
Bath BA1 1HE, UK

ISBN: 978-1-4454-3249-6

Printed in China

Designed by Terry Jeavons & Company

Notes for the Reader
This book uses imperial, metric, and US cup measurements. Follow the same units of measurement throughout; do not mix imperial and metric. All spoon measurements are level: teaspoons are assumed to be 5 ml, and tablespoons are assumed to be 15 ml. Unless otherwise stated, milk is assumed to be whole, eggs and individual vegetables such as potatoes are medium, and pepper is freshly ground black pepper.

The times given are an approximate guide only. Preparation times differ according to the techniques used by different people and the cooking times may also vary from those given as a result of the type of oven used. Optional ingredients, variations or serving suggestions have not been included in the calculations.

Recipes using raw or very lightly cooked eggs should be avoided by infants, the elderly, pregnant women, convalescents, and anyone with a chronic condition. Pregnant and breastfeeding women are advised to avoid eating peanuts and peanut products. Sufferers from nut allergies should be aware that some of the ready-prepared ingredients used in the recipes in this book may contain nuts. Always check the packaging before use.

Picture Acknowledgements
The publisher would like to thank the following for permission to reproduce copyright material on the front cover: Blueberry Smoothie © Leigh Beisch/Getty Images

SMOOTHIES & JUICES

introduction

The ancestry of smoothies can be traced back to the milkshake that was so fashionable half a century ago, but their style and phenomenal popularity are thoroughly modern. All of their aspects reflect contemporary preoccupations— they're bursting with flavor, wonderfully refreshing, nourishing and sustaining, free from preservatives and artificial coloring, incredibly quick to make, look fabulous, and kids think they're cool.

They may be made with fruit, vegetables, or a mixture of both and some include milk, yogurt, or similar products. They rarely require extra sweetening and when they do, this is often in the form

of honey rather than refined sugar. Unlike milkshakes, which are usually made with flavored syrup, smoothies always contain a high proportion of whole fruits or vegetables. The bare minimum of preparation—peeling and removing seeds, for example— not only means that smoothies are very quick to make but that nutrients are not lost and healthy dietary fiber is included in every glass.

Because they taste so delicious and are often colorful and attractive, it's easy to encourage the family to consume more fruit and vegetables, as nutritionists are constantly recommending us. This is good news for parents who may struggle with providing a healthy diet for recalcitrant children and intractable teenagers. They make great anytime-of-day drinks and a fabulous substitute for unhealthy snacks, such as potato chips and cookies. Depending on the particular ingredients, smoothies can provide an energy boost first thing in the morning and when you need to keep going later in the day, or a calming and refreshing way of winding

down and relaxing. Far more exciting than plain fruit juice, they offer a much better way to quench your thirst than commercial sodas and can form a useful part of a weight-loss plan.

Whether your taste is for sweet or savory, tangy or creamy, piquant or soothing, there's a smoothie to suit you and your good health.

energize

While nutritionists advise that breakfast is the most important meal of the day, it still remains the most neglected. In the morning rush, even a slice of toast can seem too much to prepare and teenagers, in particular, are often very negative about eating first thing in the day. Smoothies are the perfect answer—irresistible, quick to make, and packed with goodness. Some recipes in particular are ideal for kick-starting the day—citrus fruits activate the system, while bananas are powerhouses of energy that will keep you going through the whole morning.

When you feel that you're beginning to flag—in the mid-afternoon, for example—why not try a reviving smoothie instead of another cup of coffee? Replace the short-lived buzz of caffeine with a high-vitality mix of berries or an antioxidant booster of orange and red vegetables. Better still, take preemptive action and include any one of these revitalizing drinks with your lunch to prevent an energy slump later in the day.

Smoothies also make terrific after-school treats. They won't spoil the appetite for family supper, they are much healthier than potato chips or candy, and will help fortify young people to do battle with their homework.

breakfast smoothie

ingredients

SERVES 2

1 cup orange juice

$1/2$ cup plain yogurt

2 eggs

2 frozen bananas

2 small bananas, to decorate

method

1 Pour the orange juice and yogurt into a food processor or blender and process gently until combined.

2 Add the eggs and frozen bananas and process until smooth.

3 Pour the mixture into glasses and decorate with the bananas.

rise & shine juice

ingredients

SERVES 1

4 tomatoes, quartered

scant $1/2$ cup grated carrot

1 tbsp lime juice

method

1 Put the tomatoes, carrot, and lime juice into a food processor or blender and process for a few seconds until smooth.

2 Place a nylon strainer over a bowl and pour in the tomato mixture. Using a spoon, gently push as much of the liquid through the strainer as possible. Discard any seeds and pulp remaining in the strainer.

3 Pour the juice into a glass and serve at once.

banana breakfast shake

ingredients

SERVES 2

2 ripe bananas

generous $3/4$ cup low-fat yogurt

$1/2$ cup skim milk

$1/2$ tsp vanilla extract

method

1 Put the bananas, yogurt, skim milk, and vanilla extract into a food processor or blender and process until smooth.

2 Pour into glasses and serve at once.

breakfast berry smoothie

ingredients

SERVES 1–2

$1^1/_3$ cups strawberries

$^3/_4$ cup raspberries

generous $^1/_3$ cup soy milk

$^1/_2$ cup unsweetened granola

method

1 Reserve a strawberry for decoration, then process the remainder with the raspberries.

2 Pour the juice into a food processor or blender with the soy milk and granola, and process until almost smooth.

3 Pour into glasses, top each smoothie with half a strawberry, and serve.

tropical sunrise

ingredients

SERVES 1–2

1 ripe mango
1 orange
1/2 pomegranate

method

1 Remove the pit from the mango, and peel the orange. Put into a food processor or blender and process. Pour into glasses.

2 Peel the pomegranate, reserve 1 tablespoon of the seeds, and process the rest.

3 Pour into the orange and mango juice and sprinkle with the reserved pomegranate seeds.

wake-up juice

ingredients

SERVES 1–2

1 orange

1 large sprig of fresh mint, plus extra sprigs to decorate

1¹/₄ cups cubed cantaloupe melon flesh

method

1 Peel the orange, leaving on the white pith.

2 Put the orange, mint, and melon into a food processor or blender and process.

3 Pour into glasses and serve decorated with sprigs of mint.

berry brightener

ingredients

SERVES 2

1½ cups blueberries

⅔ cup cranberry juice

⅔ cup plain yogurt

honey, to taste (optional)

method

1 Put the blueberries and cranberry juice into a food processor or blender and process for 1–2 minutes, until smooth.

2 Add the yogurt and process briefly to combine. Taste and add honey, if you like. Process briefly again until thoroughly blended.

3 Pour into glasses and serve.

blueberry thrill

ingredients

SERVES 2

scant $1/2$ cup strained plain yogurt

scant $1/2$ cup water

scant 1 cup frozen blueberries, plus extra to decorate

method

1 Put the yogurt, water, and blueberries into a food processor or blender and process until smooth.

2 Pour into glasses and top with whole frozen blueberries.

tropical watermelon smoothie

ingredients

SERVES 2

1 watermelon wedge, about 1 lb 5 oz/600 g

2 small bananas, preferably Lady Finger

1 cup coconut cream

method

1 Remove and discard the seeds from the watermelon, then cut the flesh off the rind and chop coarsely. Peel and slice the bananas.

2 Put the watermelon, bananas, and coconut cream into a food processor or blender and process until combined.

3 Pour into glasses and serve.

orange & strawberry cream

ingredients

SERVES 2

$1/2$ cup plain yogurt

$3/4$ cup strawberry yogurt

$3/4$ cup orange juice

scant $1^1/4$ cups frozen strawberries

1 banana, sliced and frozen

slices of orange and whole fresh strawberries on toothpicks, to decorate

method

1 Pour the plain and strawberry yogurts into a food processor or blender and process gently. Add the orange juice and process until combined.

2 Add the strawberries and banana and process until smooth.

3 Pour the mixture into glasses and decorate with the slices of orange and strawberries.

raspberry & strawberry smoothie

ingredients

SERVES 2–4

$^{1}/_{3}$ cup raspberries

$^{1}/_{2}$ cup strawberries, halved

1 cup plain yogurt

1 cup milk

1 tsp almond extract (optional)

2–3 tbsp honey, to taste

method

1 Press the raspberries through a nylon strainer into a bowl using the back of a spoon. Discard the seeds in the strainer.

2 Put the raspberry puree, strawberries, yogurt, milk, and almond extract (if using) into a food processor or blender and process until smooth and combined.

3 Pour the smoothie into glasses, stir in honey to taste, and serve.

melon & pineapple crush

ingredients

SERVES 2

scant $^1/_2$ cup pineapple juice

4 tbsp orange juice

$^3/_4$ cup cubed galia melon

1 cup frozen pineapple chunks

4 ice cubes

slices of galia melon, to decorate

method

1 Pour the pineapple juice and orange juice into a food processor or blender and process gently until combined.

2 Add the melon, pineapple chunks, and ice cubes and process until a slushy consistency has been reached.

3 Pour the mixture into glasses and decorate with slices of melon. Serve at once.

bright eyes

ingredients

SERVES 1–2

generous 1/3 cup boiling water

1 green tea bag, or 1 tsp green tea

1 carrot

1 apple

small handful flat-leaf parsley, plus extra sprigs to garnish

method

1 Pour the boiling water onto the green tea and let stand for 4 minutes. Strain and cool slightly.

2 Place the carrot, apple, and parsley into a food processor or blender and process. Stir the juice into the tea.

3 Pour into glasses, and serve warm or cold, garnished with parsley sprigs.

fruit kefir

ingredients

SERVES 4

1 banana

1 cup strawberries, halved

1 cup peach yogurt

2 tbsp honey

1 cup apple juice, chilled

method

1 Peel the banana and slice it directly into a food processor or blender.

2 Add the strawberries, yogurt, and honey and process until smooth. With the motor running, pour in the apple juice through the hole in the lid.

3 Pour into chilled glasses and serve.

almond & banana smoothie

ingredients

SERVES 3–4

scant 1 cup whole blanched almonds

2^1/$_2$ cups dairy-free milk

2 ripe bananas, halved

1 tsp natural vanilla extract

ground cinnamon, for sprinkling

method

1 Put the almonds into a food processor or blender and process until very finely chopped. Add the milk, bananas, and vanilla extract and blend until smooth and creamy.

2 Pour into glasses and sprinkle with cinnamon.

banana, peach & strawberry smoothie

ingredients

SERVES 2

$1^1/_4$ cups whole milk or soy milk

2 tbsp plain yogurt

1 tbsp maple syrup

$^1/_2$ peeled and sliced banana

$^1/_2$ pitted, peeled, and chopped peach

3 hulled strawberries

method

1 Place all the ingredients in a food processor or blender and process until combined and frothy.

2 Pour into glasses and serve immediately.

fruity refresher

ingredients

SERVES 1–2

$1/2$ peach

1 small apple

$1/2$ kiwi

$1/4$ cup green grapes

$11/4$ cups cubed honeydew melon flesh

slices of kiwi, to garnish

method

1 Halve and pit the peach.

2 Put the peach, apple, and kiwi into a food processor or blender and process, then add the grapes and melon.

3 Stir the juice, pour into glasses, and serve, garnished with the slices of kiwi.

orchard fruit smoothie

ingredients

SERVES 2

1 ripe pear, peeled and cut into quarters
1 apple, peeled and cut into quarters
2 large red plums, halved and pitted
4 ripe dark plums, halved and pitted
generous $3/4$ cup water
slices of apple or pear, to decorate

method

1 Put the pear, apple, plums, and water into a small pan. Cover tightly, then set over medium heat and bring slowly to a boil. Take off the heat and let cool. Chill.

2 Put the fruit and water into a food processor or blender and process until smooth.

3 Pour into glasses, decorate with slices of apple or pear, and serve.

red reviver

ingredients

SERVES 1–2

2 small beets

1 carrot

1 pear

$1/2$ lime

1-inch/2.5-cm piece of fresh ginger

method

1 Place the beets and carrot into a food processor or blender and process. Then process the pear, lime, and ginger. Mix together.

2 Pour into glasses and serve.

pink zinger

ingredients

SERVES 1

1 pink grapefruit

1 orange

$^1/_2$ lemon

$^1/_2$ lime

slice of lime, to decorate

method

1 Peel the grapefruit, orange, lemon, and lime, leaving on the white pith.

2 Put the grapefruit, orange, lemon, and lime into a food processor or blender and process.

3 Pour into a glass and serve with a slice of lime on the rim of the glass.

cucumber cooler

ingredients

SERVES 1–2

1/2 cucumber

2 apples

1/2 oz/15 g fresh cilantro, leaves and stems

method

1 Cut a few long strips from the cucumber and reserve.

2 Put the apples, cilantro, and cucumber into a food processor or blender and process.

3 Pour into glasses, add the cucumber strips, and serve.

vegetable cocktail

ingredients

SERVES 2

$^1/_2$ cup carrot juice

1 lb 2 oz/500 g tomatoes, skinned, seeded, and coarsely chopped

1 tbsp lemon juice

4 celery stalks, trimmed and sliced

4 scallions, trimmed and coarsely chopped

scant $^1/_3$ cup fresh parsley

scant $^1/_3$ cup fresh mint

2 leafy celery stalks, to decorate

method

1 Put the carrot juice, tomatoes, and lemon juice into a food processor or blender and process gently until combined.

2 Add the sliced celery along with the scallions, parsley, and mint and process until smooth.

3 Pour the mixture into glasses and garnish with leafy celery stalks.

4 Serve at once.

tomato blazer

ingredients

SERVES 2

generous 2 cups tomato juice

dash of Worcestershire sauce

1 small red chile, seeded and chopped

1 scallion, trimmed and chopped

6 ice cubes, crushed

2 long, thin red chiles, cut into flowers, to decorate

method

1 To make the chile flowers, use a sharp knife to make six cuts along each chile. Place the point of the knife about $1/2$ inch/1 cm from the stem end and cut toward the tip. Put the chiles in a bowl of iced water and let stand for 25–30 minutes, or until they have spread out into flower shapes.

2 Put the tomato juice and Worcestershire sauce into a food processor or blender and process gently until combined. Add the chopped chile, scallion, and ice cubes and process until smooth.

3 Pour the mixture into glasses and garnish with the chile flowers.

carrot & red bell pepper booster

ingredients

SERVES 2

1 cup carrot juice

1 cup tomato juice

2 large red bell peppers, seeded and coarsely chopped

1 tbsp lemon juice

freshly ground black pepper

method

1 Pour the carrot juice and tomato juice into a food processor or blender and process gently until combined.

2 Add the red bell peppers and lemon juice. Season with plenty of freshly ground black pepper and process until smooth.

3 Pour the mixture into glasses and serve.

revive

From time to time, everyone in the family can feel under the weather. They may have had a horrible cold, have had trouble sleeping, be under pressure at work or school, or simply have been so busy they have been skipping meals and surviving on unhealthy snacks. Smoothies are a great way of recharging the batteries, especially as the appetite tends to wane when you're not feeling yourself.

Most people know that oranges and other citrus fruits have high levels of vitamin C that help to ward off infections, but so do tomatoes, bell peppers, and kiwis. Like bananas, kiwis are also a good source of potassium, essential for regulating blood pressure, so smoothies made with these fruits can really help prevent you from blowing your top. Replenish essential minerals with tropical fruits and cleanse the system with apples and carrots. Beet is a great, all-round pick-me-up and it's probably one of the world's best-kept secrets that it even relieves a hangover.

Growing older is a fact of life, but smoothies are literally revitalizers because most fruit and vegetables contain antioxidants with anti-aging properties. They can even help combat wrinkles and sagging skin. For example, berries, especially dark ones, such as blackberries and blueberries, are great for restoring skin tone and, as a bonus, help prevent memory loss.

banana & strawberry smoothie

ingredients

SERVES 2

1 banana, sliced

$^1/_2$ cup fresh strawberries, hulled

generous $^2/_3$ cup low-fat plain yogurt

method

1 Put the banana, strawberries, and yogurt into a food processor or blender and process for a few seconds until smooth.

2 Pour into glasses and serve at once.

papaya & banana smoothie

ingredients

SERVES 2

1 papaya

juice of 1 lime

1 large banana

$1^1/_2$ cups freshly squeezed orange juice

$^1/_4$ tsp ground ginger

method

1 Halve the papaya and scoop out and discard the gray-black seeds. Scoop out the flesh and chop coarsely, then toss with the lime juice. Peel and slice the banana.

2 Put the papaya, banana, orange juice, and ginger in a food processor or blender and process until thoroughly combined.

3 Pour into glasses and serve.

detox special

ingredients

SERVES 2

1 mango

4 kiwis

1$^1/_2$ cups pineapple juice

4 fresh mint leaves

method

1 Cut the mango into 2 thick slices as close to the pit as possible. Scoop out the flesh and chop coarsely. Cut off any flesh adhering to the pit. Peel the kiwis with a sharp knife and chop the flesh.

2 Put the mango, kiwis, pineapple juice, and mint leaves in a food processor or blender and process until thoroughly combined. Pour into glasses and serve.

tropical smoothie

ingredients

SERVES 2

1 ripe papaya, peeled, pitted, and chopped

$^1/_2$ fresh pineapple, peeled and chopped

$^2/_3$ cup soy milk

$1^1/_4$ cups soy yogurt

chopped pineapple, to decorate

method

1 Place all the ingredients in a food processor or blender and process until smooth.

2 Pour into glasses, decorate with chopped pineapple, and serve.

sunshine smoothie

ingredients

SERVES 1

2 nectarines

$1/2$ cup green seedless grapes

$1/2$ cup soy yogurt

$1/2$ tsp honey, preferably Manuka

1 tbsp sunflower seeds

method

1 Halve and pit the nectarines and place in a food processor or blender with the grapes and process.

2 Add the yogurt, honey, and half the sunflower seeds and blend until smooth.

3 Pour into a glass, sprinkle with the remaining sunflower seeds, and serve.

cherry pink

ingredients

SERVES 1–2

12 oz/350 g dark sweet cherries
1 apple
$^1/_2$ cup red grapes
$^1/_2$ lime
$^1/_4$ cup soy yogurt

method

1 Pit the cherries.

2 Place the apple, cherries, grapes, and lime into a food processor or blender and process. Whisk in the yogurt.

3 Pour into glasses and serve.

blueberry dazzler

ingredients

SERVES 2

$^3/_4$ cup apple juice

$^1/_2$ cup plain yogurt

1 banana, sliced and frozen

generous 1 cup frozen blueberries

whole fresh blueberries on toothpicks, to decorate

method

1 Pour the apple juice into a food processor or blender. Add the yogurt and process until smooth.

2 Add the banana and half of the blueberries and process well, then add the remaining blueberries and process until smooth.

3 Pour the mixture into glasses.

4 Decorate with the blueberries and serve.

pear & raspberry delight

ingredients

SERVES 2

2 large ripe Anjou pears

scant 1 cup frozen raspberries

generous ¾ cup ice-cold water

honey, to taste

raspberries on toothpicks, to decorate

method

1 Peel the pears and cut into quarters, removing the cores. Put into a food processor or blender with the raspberries and water and process until smooth.

2 Taste and sweeten with honey if the raspberries are a little sharp.

3 Pour into glasses, decorate with the raspberries, and serve.

apricot & orange smoothie

ingredients

SERVES 2

scant 1 cup dried apricots

1 cup boiling water

juice of 4 medium oranges

2 tbsp plain yogurt and 1 tsp soft dark brown sugar, to decorate

method

1 Put the apricots in a bowl and pour the boiling water over them. Let them soak overnight.

2 In the morning, put the apricots and their soaking water into a food processor or blender and process until pureed. Add the orange juice and process until combined.

3 Pour into glasses and top with the yogurt and the brown sugar.

berry booster

ingredients

SERVES 1

2 tbsp blueberries

generous $1/2$ cup raspberries, thawed if frozen

1 tsp honey

scant 1 cup live or bio yogurt

1 heaping tbsp crushed ice

1 tbsp sesame seeds

method

1 Put the blueberries into a food processor or blender and process for 1 minute.

2 Add the raspberries, honey, and yogurt and process for an additional minute.

3 Add the ice and sesame seeds and process again for an additional minute.

4 Pour into a glass and serve at once.

black & blue

ingredients

SERVES 2

generous 3/4 cup cultivated blackberries

scant 1 cup blueberries

scant 1/2 cup ice-cold water

2/3 cup plain yogurt

method

1 Put the blackberries, blueberries, water, and yogurt into a food processor or blender and process until smooth.

2 Pour into glasses and serve.

apple, carrot & cucumber juice

ingredients

SERVES 1

1 apple, unpeeled, cored, and chopped

1 carrot, peeled and chopped

$^1/_2$ cucumber, chopped

pieces of carrot, cucumber, and apple on a toothpick, to decorate

method

1 Place the ingredients in a food processor or blender and process.

2 Pour into a glass, decorate with the carrot, cucumber, and apple, and serve.

guava goodness

ingredients

SERVES 2

14 oz/400 g canned guavas, drained

1 cup ice-cold milk

method

1 Place the guavas into a food processor or blender and pour in the milk. Process until well blended.

2 Strain into glasses to remove the hard seeds. Serve.

24 carrot

ingredients

SERVES 2

handful of cracked ice

2 carrots, coarsely chopped

4 oz/100 g canned pineapple pieces in juice, drained

$^3/_4$ cup pineapple juice, chilled

strips of cucumber, to decorate

method

1 Put the ice into a food processor or blender, add the carrots, pineapple pieces, and pineapple juice, and process until slushy.

2 Pour into glasses and decorate with strips of cucumber.

carrot cocktail

ingredients

SERVES 1

3 oz/85 g raw carrots, peeled and roughly chopped

1$^1/_2$ medium pineapples, roughly chopped

1 tsp lemon juice

1 tbsp honey

ice

sprig of parsley or mint, to decorate

method

1 Place the carrots, pineapple, lemon juice, and honey in a food processor or blender and process until smooth.

2 Serve over ice with a sprig of parsley or mint.

mint & cucumber refresher

ingredients

SERVES 1

few sprigs mint

1 tsp confectioners' sugar

juice 1 lime

1-inch/2-cm piece cucumber, thinly sliced

your favorite sparkling water, chilled

ice cubes

method

1 Chop a few mint leaves and mix with the sugar.

2 Rub a little lime juice around the rim of a pretty glass and dip in the minted sugar. Let dry.

3 Mix the rest of the lime juice, cucumber, and mint—some chopped and some whole—in a pitcher and chill.

4 Pour the lime and cucumber into the prepared glass, fill with chilled water to taste, and serve.

sweet & sour smoothie

ingredients

SERVES 2

1 cup freshly squeezed orange juice

1 cup cooked beet, chopped, plus extra to decorate

5 tbsp plain yogurt

$2/3$ cup water

salt (optional)

method

1 Put the orange juice, beet, and yogurt into a food processor or blender and add water. Process until smooth and thoroughly combined.

2 Pour the smoothie into a chilled pitcher and stir in salt to taste (if using).

3 Decorate with chopped beet and serve.

apple & celery revitalizer

ingredients

SERVES 2

1 apple, peeled, cored, and diced

1 cup chopped celery

1¼ cups milk

pinch of sugar (optional)

salt (optional)

strips of celery, to decorate

method

1 Put the apple, celery, and milk in a food processor or blender and process until thoroughly combined.

2 Stir in a pinch of sugar and some salt (if using).

3 Pour into glasses, decorate with strips of celery, and serve.

the reviver

ingredients

SERVES 1–2

$^1/_2$ galia melon

3 celery stalks

generous $^3/_4$ cup blackberries

1 kiwi

method

1 Peel the melon and cut into chunks.

2 Put into a food processor or blender with 1 celery stalk, the blackberries, and the kiwi.

3 Process all the ingredients together, then pour into glasses and serve with the remaining celery stalks to stir.

rapid recharge

ingredients

SERVES 1–2

1 small zucchini

1 celery stalk

1¹/₂ oz/40 g baby leaf spinach

1¹/₂ oz/40 g alfalfa sprouts

2 apples

1 tsp alfalfa sprouts, to decorate

method

1 Trim the zucchini and put into a food processor or blender with the celery, add the spinach and the alfalfa, then the apples.

2 Process all the ingredients, then pour into glasses.

3 Decorate with a few alfalfa sprouts and serve.

red bell pepper reactor

ingredients

SERVES 2

1 cup carrot juice

1 cup tomato juice

2 large red bell peppers, seeded and coarsely chopped

1 tbsp lemon juice

freshly ground black pepper

strips of shredded carrot, to decorate

method

1 Pour the carrot juice and tomato juice into a food processor or blender and process gently until combined.

2 Add the red bell peppers and lemon juice. Season with plenty of freshly ground black pepper and process until smooth.

3 Pour the mixture into glasses, decorate with strips of shredded carrot, and serve.

on the beat

ingredients

SERVES 2

generous 1 cup chopped, cooked beet

$^1/_2$ cup orange juice, chilled

5 tbsp plain yogurt, chilled

$^2/_3$ cup mineral water, chilled

salt

slices of orange, to decorate

method

1 Put the beet, orange juice, yogurt, and water into a food processor or blender and season to taste with salt.

2 Process until smooth, pour into glasses, and serve decorated with the slices of orange.

refresh

On a hot summer's day or after a burst of vigorous exercise, a long, thirst-quenching cooler is just what's needed rather than a creamy and substantial smoothie. Fortunately, there are fruits so full of juice and with such naturally refreshing flavors that they fit the bill exactly. Apart from the citrus family, watermelon, pineapple, mango, and pomegranate instantly spring to mind. Sweet enough to delight the taste buds without being sticky or cloying, they mix and match into deliciously fresh-flavored summer drinks.

Sometimes whole fruits are combined with pure juice for instant rehydration, but this does not in any way detract from the health-giving, restorative properties of refresher smoothies. A baking hot day can leave you feeling limp and lethargic, so it's important to re-establish the body's balance as well as replace the fluid lost through sweating. Equally, a restorative smoothie following an energetic session of exercise will help maintain that satisfying feeling of invigoration. Fruits rich in calcium and magnesium, such as oranges and apricots, stimulate cell repair, while apples, mangoes, and passion fruit help replace lost energy.

It's worth remembering to put fruit juice and glasses in the refrigerator to chill in advance so that when you mix your drink it is pleasantly cool. Adding ice cubes would work, too, of course, but would also dilute the flavor.

raspberry & apple quencher

ingredients

SERVES 2

8 ice cubes, crushed

2 tbsp raspberry syrup

generous 2 cups chilled apple juice

pieces of apple and whole raspberries on toothpicks, to decorate

method

1 Divide the crushed ice between the glasses and pour over the raspberry syrup.

2 Fill each glass with the apple juice and stir well.

3 Decorate with the raspberries and pieces of apple and serve.

watermelon refresher

ingredients

SERVES 2

1 wedge of watermelon, weighing about 12 oz/350 g

ice cubes

slices of watermelon, to decorate

method

1 Cut the rind off the watermelon. Chop the watermelon into chunks, discarding any seeds.

2 Put the watermelon chunks into a food processor or blender and process until smooth.

3 Place ice cubes in the glasses. Pour the watermelon mixture over the ice and serve decorated with slices of melon.

perky pineapple

ingredients

SERVES 4

handful of cracked ice

2 bananas

1 cup pineapple juice, chilled

$^1/_2$ cup lime juice

slices of pineapple, to decorate

method

1 Put the cracked ice into the food processor or blender. Peel the bananas and slice directly into the blender. Add the pineapple and lime juice and process until smooth.

2 Pour into chilled glasses, decorate with slices of pineapple, and serve.

melon & mango tango

ingredients

SERVES 2

1 cantaloupe melon, halved and seeded

2$\frac{1}{2}$ cups mango juice

2 tbsp fresh orange juice

slices of orange, to decorate

method

1 Scoop out the melon flesh with a spoon straight into the food processor or blender. Add the mango and orange juices and process until smooth.

2 Pour into chilled glasses, decorate with slices of orange, and serve.

blueberry nectar

ingredients

SERVES 1–2

1 pear

1 cup blueberries

$1/2$ cup soy yogurt

$1/2$ tsp agave syrup

2 tsp toasted, slivered almonds

method

1 Put the pear and blueberries into a food processor or blender and process.

2 Add the yogurt and agave syrup and process until smooth and bubbly.

3 Pour into a glass, sprinkle with the almonds, and serve.

fresh & fruity

ingredients

SERVES 1–2

$1/2$ small pineapple

generous $1/2$ cup blackberries

generous $1/2$ cup blueberries

1 tsp goji berries, roughly chopped, to decorate

method

1 Cut the pineapple into chunks and put into a food processor or blender with the blackberries and blueberries. Process.

2 Pour into a glass and sprinkle with the chopped goji berries.

apricot buzz

ingredients

SERVES 1–2

6 apricots

1 orange

1 fresh lemongrass stalk

3/4-inch/2-cm piece of fresh ginger

method

1 Halve and pit the apricots. Peel the orange, leaving some of the white pith. Cut the lemongrass into chunks.

2 Place the apricots, orange, lemongrass, and ginger in a food processor or blender and process all the ingredients together.

3 Pour into glasses and serve.

watermelon sunset

ingredients

SERVES 4

1 watermelon, halved
6 tbsp fresh ruby grapefruit juice
6 tbsp fresh orange juice
dash of lime juice
slices of watermelon, to decorate

method

1 Remove the seeds in the melon if you are unable to find a seedless one. Scoop the flesh into a food processor or blender and add the grapefruit juice, orange juice, and a dash of lime juice.

2 Process until smooth and pour into glasses. Decorate with the slices of watermelon and serve.

apple cooler

ingredients

SERVES 2

2 apples, peeled and roughly chopped

$1/3$ cup strawberries, hulled

juice of 4 oranges

sugar, to taste

slices of apple, to decorate

method

1 Put the apples, strawberries, and orange juice into a food processor or blender and process until smooth.

2 Taste and sweeten with sugar if necessary.

3 Decorate with slices of apple and serve at once.

lemon surprise

ingredients

SERVES 2

juice of 1 lemon

1 tbsp chopped fresh parsley

scant 2 cups sparkling mineral water

2–3 tsp sugar

method

1 Put the lemon juice, parsley, and mineral water into a food processor or blender and process until combined.

2 Add the sugar through a feeder tube, and process for 30 seconds or more.

3 Pour into glasses and serve.

maidenly mimosa

ingredients

SERVES 2

3/4 cup freshly squeezed orange juice

3/4 cup sparkling white grape juice

method

1 Divide the orange juice between chilled wine glasses or champagne flutes.

2 Fill with the grape juice and serve.

pomegranate passion

ingredients

SERVES 2

2 ripe pomegranates

1 passion fruit

1 tbsp honey

2 glasses full of crushed ice

method

1 Cut the pomegranates in half and extract the juice with an old-fashioned lemon squeezer.

2 Halve the passion fruit and strain the pulp into a small bowl. Mix in the pomegranate juice and honey.

3 Pour over the crushed ice and serve.

melon & mint cooler

ingredients

SERVES 2

1 cantaloupe melon

1 tbsp chopped fresh mint

1 tbsp chopped preserved ginger

$1/2$–$2/3$ cup mineral water

method

1 Halve the melon and scoop out and discard the seeds. Scoop out the flesh and chop coarsely.

2 Put the melon, mint, and ginger into a food processor or blender and process until smooth and thoroughly combined. With the motor running, add the mineral water, a little at a time, until the mixture reaches the consistency that suits you.

3 Pour into glasses and serve.

pineapple crush

ingredients

SERVES 2

scant $^1/_2$ cup pineapple juice

4 tbsp orange juice

$^3/_4$ cup cubed galia melon

generous $^1/_2$ cup frozen pineapple chunks

4 ice cubes

slices of orange, to decorate

method

1 Pour the pineapple juice and orange juice into a food processor or blender and process gently until combined.

2 Add the melon, pineapple chunks, and ice cubes, and process until a slushy consistency has been reached.

3 Pour the mixture into glasses and decorate with slices of orange. Serve at once.

passionate juice fizz

ingredients

SERVES 1–2

1 pomegranate

$^1/_2$ small orange

4 passion fruit

$^1/_3$–$^1/_2$ cup sparkling mineral water

method

1 Peel the rind from the pomegranate and peel the orange, leaving on the white pith. Scoop the flesh from the passion fruit.

2 Put the pomegranate with the orange and pulp from 3 passion fruit into a food processor or blender and process.

3 Pour into a glass and stir in the remaining passion fruit pulp. Fill with the mineral water and serve.

strawberry & pineapple refresher

ingredients

SERVES 2

1 cup frozen strawberries

1¼ cups pineapple juice

1 tbsp superfine sugar

wedges of pineapple, to decorate

method

1 Put the strawberries, pineapple juice, and sugar into a food processor or blender and blend until smooth.

2 Pour into glasses, decorate with wedges of pineapple, and serve.

black grape fizz

ingredients

SERVES 2

scant 1 cup black grapes, seeded or seedless

generous $^3/_4$ cup sparkling mineral water

2 large scoops of lemon sherbet

slices of lime, to decorate

method

1 Put the grapes, mineral water, and lemon sherbet into a food processor or blender and process until smooth.

2 Pour into glasses and decorate with slices of lime. Serve immediately.

homemade lemonade

ingredients

SERVES 2

$^2/_3$ cup water

6 tbsp sugar

1 tsp grated lemon rind

$^1/_2$ cup lemon juice

6 ice cubes

sparkling water, to serve

granulated sugar and slices of lemon, to decorate

method

1 Put the water, sugar, and grated lemon rind into a small pan and bring to a boil, stirring constantly. Continue to boil, stirring, for 5 minutes.

2 Remove from the heat and let cool to room temperature. Stir in the lemon juice, then transfer to a pitcher and cover with plastic wrap. Chill in the refrigerator for at least 2 hours.

3 When the lemonade has almost finished chilling, take two glasses and rub the rims with a wedge of lemon, then dip them in sugar to frost. Put the ice cubes into the glasses.

4 Remove the lemon syrup from the refrigerator, then pour it over the ice and fill with sparkling water. The ratio should be one part lemon syrup to three parts sparkling water. Stir well to mix. Decorate with sugar and slices of fresh lemon and serve.

soothe

Life is so hectic nowadays that even when we do have some time to ourselves, it is often difficult to relax and unwind. Most of us have known nights when we fall exhausted into bed but the mind keeps on going, churning over the day's concerns and worrying about tomorrow's. Let go with a soothing smoothie, releasing the tension and calming both mind and body, confident that every restorative sip is doing you good. It's not just healthier than a glass of wine—alcohol depletes the body's supplies of important vitamins and minerals—but more effective, too.

These smoothies do far more than just replace the energy used up during the day. They are great stress busters in their own right. Research has shown that a pressurized lifestyle actually robs the body of essential vitamins and minerals, so it is important to replace these. In addition, an increased intake of vitamin C reduces the levels of stress hormones in the blood and actually lifts the spirits. A smoothie made with citrus fruits, cantaloupe melon, berries, or kiwis, for example, is an easy way to achieve this and more fun to swallow than supplements. It's natural sweetness will help you get a good night's sleep, too.

pear, orange & ginger reviver

ingredients

SERVES 2

2 large ripe bartlett or similar juicy pears
juice of 4 medium oranges
4 cubes candied ginger

method

1 Peel the pears and cut into quarters, removing the cores. Put into a food processor or blender with the orange juice and the candied ginger and process until smooth.

2 Pour into glasses and serve.

sunrise crush

ingredients

SERVES 4

1 medium ripe pineapple
5 oranges, halved
ice cubes, to serve

method

1 Slice off the bottom of the pineapple and stand it upright on a board. Remove the spiky skin, then cut into six long pieces.

2 Puree the pineapple in a food processor or blender.

3 Squeeze the oranges, then mix the orange and pineapple juices together in a pitcher.

4 Pour the juice into glasses. Top with some ice cubes.

summer fruit slush

ingredients

SERVES 2

4 tbsp orange juice

1 tbsp lime juice

scant $^1/_2$ cup sparkling water

$2^1/_3$ cups frozen summer fruits (such as blueberries, raspberries, blackberries, and strawberries)

4 ice cubes

method

1 Pour the orange juice, lime juice, and sparkling water into a food processor or blender and process gently until combined.

2 Add the summer fruits and ice cubes and process until a slushy consistency has been reached.

3 Pour the mixture into glasses and serve.

forest fruit smoothie

ingredients

SERVES 2

1^1/$_2$ cups orange juice

1 banana, sliced and frozen

3 cups frozen forest fruits (such as blueberries, raspberries, and blackberries)

slices of orange, to decorate

method

1 Pour the orange juice into a food processor or blender. Add the banana and half of the forest fruits and process until smooth.

2 Add the remaining forest fruits and process until smooth.

3 Pour the mixture into tall glasses and decorate the rims with slices of orange. Serve.

passionate magic

ingredients

SERVES 1–2

2 peaches

generous $1/2$ cup red grapes

$3/4$ cup strawberries

1 passion fruit

seeds from $1/2$ vanilla bean

method

1 Halve and pit the peaches, put into a food processor or blender with the grapes and strawberries, and process.

2 Halve the passion fruit and scoop out the flesh, scrape the seeds from the vanilla bean, and stir both into the juice.

3 Pour into glasses and serve.

mango & orange smoothie

ingredients

SERVES 2

1 large ripe mango
juice of 2 medium oranges
3 scoops of mango sherbet
strips of orange zest, to decorate

method

1 Place the mango on a cutting board and cut lengthwise through the flesh as close to the large flat central pit as possible. Turn it over and do the same thing on the other side of the pit. Remove the peel and coarsely chop the flesh before placing in a food processor or blender.

2 Add the orange juice and sherbet and process until smooth.

3 Serve at once, decorated with strips of orange zest.

honeydew

ingredients

SERVES 2

9 oz/250 g honeydew melon

1¹/₄ cups sparkling mineral water

2 tbsp honey

red currant clusters, to decorate

method

1 Cut the rind off the melon. Chop the melon into chunks, discarding any seeds.

2 Put into a food processor or blender with the water and honey and process until smooth.

3 Pour into glasses and decorate with clusters of red currants.

melon refresher

ingredients

SERVES 2

1 cup plain yogurt

generous $1/2$ cup cubed galia melon, cut into chunks

generous $1/2$ cup cubed cantaloupe melon, cut into chunks

generous $1/2$ cup cubed watermelon, cut into chunks

6 ice cubes, crushed

wedges of melon, to decorate

method

1 Pour the yogurt into a food processor or blender. Add the galia melon chunks and process until smooth.

2 Add the cantaloupe melon and watermelon chunks along with the ice cubes and process until smooth.

3 Pour the mixture into glasses and decorate with wedges of melon.

4 Serve at once.

banana & apple booster

ingredients

SERVES 2

1 cup apple juice

$1/2$ tsp cinnamon

2 tsp grated fresh ginger

2 bananas, sliced and frozen

chunks of apple on toothpicks, to decorate

method

1 Pour the apple juice into a food processor or blender. Add the cinnamon and ginger and process gently until combined.

2 Add the bananas and process until smooth. Pour the mixture into glasses and decorate with the apple. Serve at once.

cherry sour

ingredients

SERVES 2

9 oz/250 g bottled morello cherries

$^2/_3$ cup strained plain yogurt

sugar, to taste

cherries on toothpicks, to decorate

method

1 Put the cherries with their bottling liquid into a food processor or blender with the yogurt, then process until smooth.

2 Taste and sweeten with sugar if necessary.

3 Pour into glasses, decorate with the cherries, and serve.

cherry kiss

ingredients

SERVES 2

8 ice cubes, crushed

2 tbsp cherry syrup

generous 2 cups sparkling water

maraschino cherries on long swizzle sticks, to decorate

method

1 Divide the crushed ice between two glasses and pour over the cherry syrup.

2 Fill each glass with sparkling water. Decorate with the maraschino cherries and serve.

cranberry energizer

ingredients

SERVES 2

1^1/$_4$ cups cranberry juice

scant ^{1}/$_2$ cup orange juice

1^1/$_4$ cups fresh raspberries

1 tbsp lemon juice

slices and spirals of orange, to decorate

method

1 Pour the cranberry juice and orange juice into a food processor or blender and process gently until combined. Add the raspberries and lemon juice and process until smooth.

2 Pour the mixture into glasses and decorate with the slices and spirals of orange. Serve at once.

black currant bracer

ingredients

SERVES 2

$2/3$ cup frozen black currants

4 scoops of black currant sherbet

scant $1/2$ cup sour cream

2 tbsp black currant syrup, plus extra for drizzling

1 tbsp water

sugar, to taste

a few mint leaves and whole blackberries, to decorate

method

1 Put the black currants, sherbet, sour cream, syrup, and water into a food processor or blender and process until smooth. Taste and sweeten with a little sugar if necessary.

2 Pour into glasses. Drizzle over some syrup, decorate with the mint leaves and blackberries, and serve.

kiwi cooler

ingredients

SERVES 2

4 ripe kiwis, peeled and cut into fourths

generous $3/4$ cup traditional sparkling lemonade

2 large scoops of ice cream or sherbet, to decorate

method

1 Put the kiwis and lemonade into a food processor or blender and process until smooth.

2 Pour into glasses and top with a scoop of ice cream or sherbet.

3 Serve at once.

white grape elderflower foam

ingredients

SERVES 2

generous $^1/_2$ cup white grapes, deseeded or seedless

generous $^3/_4$ cup sparkling mineral water

2 large scoops of frozen yogurt

$1^1/_2$ tbsp elderflower syrup

white grapes, to decorate

method

1 Put the grapes, mineral water, frozen yogurt, and elderflower syrup into a food processor or blender and process until smooth.

2 Pour into glasses, add a few grapes, and serve immediately.

kiwi juice box

ingredients

SERVES 1–2

1 kiwi

1 apple

$1/2$ cup seedless white grapes

ice (optional)

method

1 Put the kiwi and apple into a food processor or blender and process. Then add the grapes and process.

2 Pour into glasses and serve just as it is, or pour over ice.

pineapple tango

ingredients

SERVES 2

$1/2$ cup pineapple juice

juice of 1 lemon

scant $1/2$ cup water

3 tbsp brown sugar

generous $3/4$ cup plain yogurt

1 peach, cut into chunks and frozen

$3/4$ cup frozen pineapple chunks

wedges of fresh pineapple, to decorate

method

1 Pour the pineapple juice, lemon juice, and water into a food processor or blender. Add the sugar and yogurt and process until blended.

2 Add the peach and pineapple chunks and process until smooth.

3 Pour the mixture into glasses and decorate the rims with wedges of fresh pineapple.

4 Serve at once.

elderflower & pear smoothie

ingredients

SERVES 2

4 small firm pears

2 heads of elderflowers, freshly picked (or a dash of syrup)

1 strip of lemon zest

1 tbsp soft brown sugar

4 tbsp water

generous $3/4$ cup low-fat milk

cats' tongues or similar cookies, to serve

method

1 Peel the pears and cut into fourths, discarding the cores. Place in a pan with the elderflowers, a strip of lemon zest, the sugar, and water. Cover tightly and simmer until the pears are very soft. Let cool.

2 Discard the elderflowers and lemon zest. Put the pears, cooking liquid, and milk into a food processor or blender and process until smooth.

3 Serve immediately with cats' tongues.

cold comforter

ingredients

SERVES 1–2

1 white grapefruit

1 orange

1 kiwi

15 drops echinacea tincture

thinly pared twists of orange zest, to decorate

method

1 Peel the grapefruit and orange, leaving on some of the white pith.

2 Put the grapefruit, orange, and kiwi into a food processor or blender and process. Stir in the echinacea drops and pour into glasses.

3 Add a twist of orange zest to each and serve.

one for the girls

ingredients

SERVES 1

1 apple

1 large carrot

1 celery stalk

$^1/_2$ fennel bulb

$^1/_2$ tsp flax seeds

method

1 Put the apple, carrot, celery, and fennel into a food processor or blender and process.

2 Pour into a glass and sprinkle with flax seeds to serve.

iced fruit boost

ingredients

SERVES 1–2

1/2 lemon

2 apples

3 oz/85 g pitted prunes

2 pears

freshly grated nutmeg, to decorate

method

1 Peel the lemon, leaving on a layer of white pith.

2 Put the apples, lemon, prunes, and pears into a food processor or blender and process.

3 Pour into glasses, sprinkle with grated nutmeg, and serve.

green goddess

ingredients

SERVES 1–2

1/2 galia melon

3 oz/85 g baby leaf spinach

2 large sprigs of mint

2 large sprigs of flat-leaf parsley

ice

fresh mint sprigs, to decorate

method

1 Cut the outer hard rind from the melon, leaving the inner green layer, and cut into chunks.

2 Put half of the melon into a food processor or blender, then put in the spinach and herbs, and top with the remaining melon.

3 Process the ingredients then pour into glasses over ice. Add a sprig of mint to each and serve.

blood orange sparkler

ingredients

SERVES 2

generous 1 cup blood (ruby) orange juice

$^3/_4$ cup strawberries

$^3/_4$ cup raspberries

$^1/_4$ cup sparkling mineral water

method

1 Put the blood orange juice, strawberries, raspberries, and mineral water into a food processor or blender and process until smooth. Strain the mixture to remove the seeds, if preferred.

2 Pour into glasses and serve.

hot black currant toddy

ingredients

SERVES 1

1 apple

7 oz/200 g black currants

scant $^1/_2$ cup boiling water

1 tsp whipped honey, preferably Manuka

method

1 Put the apple and the black currants into a food processor or blender and process.

2 Add the honey to the boiling water and stir to dissolve, then stir in the juice.

3 Pour into a glass and serve immediately.

bliss

We all need a treat now and again, and an occasional moment of self-indulgence is good for the soul. These smoothies allow you to yield to the enticing lure of your favorite decadent pleasure once in a while without going completely over the top.

Of course, fruit smoothies still feature, but here they are combined in deliciously rich and creamy mixtures or mouthwatering medleys of luscious sweetness. Everyone's top temptation—chocolate—takes a starring role in several fabulous concoctions, sometimes sharing center stage with that other delicious addiction—coffee.

Not all these blissful smoothies are such guilty pleasures. Rather, they are unusual drinks that hit the spot when you feel like something a little different and can't think exactly what. If you want to spice up a dull evening, don't head for the cocktail shaker—set off for the blender instead and try some tasty piquant treats with ginger or peppermint. Set a tropical mood with a velvety coconut smoothie or a garden party atmosphere with strawberries and cream.

Bliss is not just for adults—the younger members of the family will love these special smoothies, too. They're probably not for everyday drinking but would be the perfect choice for a birthday party or other special occasion.

strawberries & cream milkshake

ingredients

SERVES 2

1 cup frozen strawberries

scant $^1/_2$ cup light cream

generous $^3/_4$ cup whole milk

1 tbsp superfine sugar

mint leaves, to decorate

method

1 Put the strawberries, cream, milk, and sugar into a food processor or blender and process until smooth.

2 Pour into glasses and serve decorated with mint leaves.

chocolate milkshake

ingredients

SERVES 2

$2/3$ cup milk

2 tbsp chocolate syrup

$1/3$ cup chocolate ice cream

grated chocolate, to decorate

method

1 Pour the milk and chocolate syrup into a food processor or blender and process gently until combined.

2 Add the chocolate ice cream and process until smooth. Pour the mixture into glasses and scatter the grated chocolate over the shakes.

3 Serve at once.

spiced banana milkshake

ingredients

SERVES 2

1$^1/_4$ cups milk

$^1/_2$ tsp allspice

generous $^3/_4$ cup banana ice cream

2 bananas, sliced and frozen

pinch of allspice, to decorate

method

1 Pour the milk into a food processor or blender and add the allspice. Add half of the banana ice cream and process gently until combined. Add the remaining ice cream and process until well blended.

2 When the mixture is well combined, add the bananas and process until smooth.

3 Pour the mixture into glasses, add a pinch of allspice to decorate, and serve.

perfect plum shake

ingredients

SERVES 2

9 oz/250 g ripe plums

generous $3/4$ cup water

1 tbsp golden granulated sugar

4 scoops of frozen yogurt (plain) or ice cream

plums, cut in half, and 2 Italian almond or pistachio biscotti, crumbled, to decorate

method

1 Put the plums, water, and sugar into a small pan. Cover tightly and simmer for about 15 minutes, or until the plums have split and are very soft. Let cool.

2 Strain off the liquid into a food processor or blender and add the frozen yogurt or ice cream. Process until smooth and frothy.

3 Pour into glasses and decorate the rims with whole or halved plums. Sprinkle with the crumbled biscotti and serve.

creamy maple shake

ingredients

SERVES 2

$2/3$ cup milk

2 tbsp maple syrup

3 cups vanilla ice cream

1 tbsp almond extract

chopped almonds, to decorate

method

1 Pour the milk and maple syrup into a food processor or blender and process gently until combined.

2 Add the ice cream and almond extract and process until smooth.

3 Pour the mixture into glasses, scatter the chopped nuts over the shakes, and serve.

kiwi & lime shake

ingredients

SERVES 2

$^2/_3$ cup milk

juice of 2 limes

2 kiwis, chopped

1 tbsp sugar

3 cups vanilla ice cream

slices of kiwi fruit, and strips of lime peel, to decorate

method

1 Pour the milk and lime juice into a food processor or blender and process gently until combined.

2 Add the kiwis and sugar and process gently, then add the ice cream and process until smooth.

3 Pour the mixture into glasses and decorate with slices of kiwis and strips of lime peel. Serve at once.

peach & orange milkshake

ingredients

SERVES 2

scant $^1/_2$ cup milk

$^1/_2$ cup peach yogurt

scant $^1/_2$ cup orange juice

1 cup canned peach slices, drained

6 ice cubes

method

1 Pour the milk, yogurt, and orange juice into a food processor or blender and process gently until combined.

2 Add the peach slices and ice cubes and process until smooth. Pour the mixture into glasses.

smooth nectarine shake

ingredients

SERVES 2

1 cup milk

1³/₄ cups lemon sherbet

1 ripe mango, pitted and diced

2 ripe nectarines, pitted and diced

thin wedges of nectarine, to decorate

method

1 Pour the milk into a food processor or blender, then add half of the lemon sherbet and process gently until combined. Add the remaining sherbet and process until smooth.

2 When the mixture is thoroughly blended, gradually add the mango and nectarines and process until smooth.

3 Pour the mixture into glasses, decorate with thin wedges of nectarine, and serve.

pink ginger shake

ingredients

SERVES 1

7 oz/200 g pink rhubarb

1 orange

3/4-inch/2-cm piece fresh ginger

1/4 cup soy milk

pinch of ground ginger, to decorate

method

1 Trim the rhubarb and cut into chunks. Peel the orange, leaving some of the white pith.

2 Put the rhubarb, orange, and ginger into a food processor or blender and process. Add the soy milk and shake or whisk to mix.

3 Pour into a glass, sprinkle with ginger, and serve.

tropical storm

ingredients

SERVES 2

1 cup milk

scant $1/2$ cup coconut milk

generous 1 cup vanilla ice cream

2 bananas, sliced and frozen

scant $1^1/2$ cups canned pineapple chunks, drained

1 papaya, seeded and diced

grated coconut, to decorate

method

1 Pour the milk and coconut milk into a food processor or blender and process gently until combined. Add half of the ice cream and process gently, then add the remaining ice cream and process until smooth.

2 Add the bananas and process well, then add the pineapple chunks and papaya and process until smooth.

3 Pour the mixture into glasses, scatter the grated coconut over the shakes, and serve.

plum fluff

ingredients

SERVES 2

4 medium ripe plums, pitted

generous $3/4$ cup ice-cold milk

2 scoops of luxury vanilla ice cream

crumbly oat cookies, to serve

method

1 Put the plums, milk, and ice cream into a food processor or blender and process until smooth and frothy.

2 Pour into glasses and serve at once with crumbly oat cookies.

peach bliss

ingredients

SERVES 2

$^3/_4$ cup milk

1 cup canned peach slices, drained

2 fresh apricots, chopped

$2^2/_3$ cups fresh strawberries, hulled and sliced

2 bananas, sliced and frozen

slices of nectarine, strawberries, and banana on toothpicks, to decorate

method

1 Pour the milk into a food processor or blender. Add the peach slices and process gently until combined. Add the apricots and process gently until combined.

2 Add the strawberries and banana slices and process until smooth.

3 Pour the mixture into glasses and decorate with the nectarine, strawberries, and banana. Serve at once.

black & white smoothie

ingredients

SERVES 2

$3/4$ cup black cherries

3 large scoops of luxury white chocolate ice cream

$2/3$ cup milk

method

1 Halve and pit the black cherries. Put these into a food processor or blender and process until pureed.

2 Add the ice cream and milk and process briefly to mix well.

3 Pour into glasses and serve.

coconut cream

ingredients

SERVES 2

1¹/₂ cups pineapple juice

¹/₃ cup coconut milk

generous 1 cup vanilla ice cream

1 cup frozen pineapple chunks

2 tbsp grated fresh coconut, to decorate

2 scooped-out coconut shells, optional, to serve

method

1 Pour the pineapple juice and coconut milk into a food processor or blender. Add the ice cream and process until smooth.

2 Add the pineapple chunks and process until smooth.

3 Pour the mixture into scooped-out coconut shells, or glasses, and decorate with grated fresh coconut.

peppermint refresher

ingredients

SERVES 2

$2/3$ cup milk

2 tbsp peppermint syrup

3 cups peppermint ice cream

sprigs of fresh mint, to decorate

method

1 Pour the milk and peppermint syrup into a food processor or blender and process gently until combined.

2 Add the peppermint ice cream and process until smooth.

3 Pour the mixture into glasses and decorate with sprigs of fresh mint.

raspberry ripple rice cream

ingredients

SERVES 2

generous ³/₄ cup frozen raspberries

1¹/₄ cups rice milk or soy milk

method

1 Put the raspberries and half the rice milk into a food processor or blender and process until smooth.

2 Strain into a pitcher and carefully stir through the remaining rice milk to create a marbled effect.

3 Pour into glasses and serve.

going bananas

ingredients

SERVES 4

1 large ripe mango
4 bananas, peeled and cut into chunks
1³/₄ cups plain yogurt
1³/₄ cups coconut milk

method

1 Cut both sides of the mango away from the pit in the middle. Scoop out the flesh with a spoon.

2 Slice the bananas into chunks and place in a food processor or blender with the mango, yogurt, and coconut milk. Put on the lid and blend until smooth.

3 Pour the smoothie into glasses and serve.

midsummer smoothie

ingredients

SERVES 2

generous $^3/_4$ cup strawberries

generous $^3/_4$ cup raspberries

scant $^1/_2$ cup blueberries

1 ripe passion fruit

$^2/_3$ cup low-fat milk

vanilla and strawberry ice cream, to decorate

method

1 Lightly rinse the strawberries, raspberries, and blueberries, and scoop out the passion fruit pulp. Place all the fruits in a food processor or blender and blend for 1 minute. Add the milk and blend again.

2 Pour into glasses and serve with a scoop of vanilla and strawberry ice cream on top of each.

iced coffee & chocolate crush

ingredients

SERVES 2

1³/₄ cups milk

generous ³/₄ cup coffee syrup

scant ¹/₂ cup peppermint syrup

1 tbsp chopped fresh mint leaves

4 ice cubes

grated chocolate, and sprigs of fresh mint, to decorate

method

1 Pour the milk, coffee syrup, and peppermint syrup into a food processor or blender and process gently until combined.

2 Add the mint and ice cubes and process until a slushy consistency has been reached.

3 Pour the mixture into glasses. Scatter over the grated chocolate, then decorate with sprigs of fresh mint and serve.

mocha cream

ingredients

SERVES 2

generous $^3/_4$ cup milk

scant $^1/_4$ cup light cream

1 tbsp brown sugar

2 tbsp unsweetened cocoa

1 tbsp coffee syrup or instant coffee powder

6 ice cubes

whipped cream and grated chocolate, to decorate

method

1 Put the milk, cream, and sugar into a food processor or blender and process gently until combined.

2 Add the cocoa and coffee syrup or powder and process well, then add the ice cubes and process until smooth.

3 Pour the mixture into glasses. Top with whipped cream, then scatter the grated chocolate over the drinks and serve.

coffee banana cooler

ingredients

SERVES 2

1¼ cups milk

4 tbsp instant coffee powder

generous 1 cup vanilla ice cream

2 bananas, sliced and frozen

method

1 Pour the milk into a food processor or blender, then add the coffee powder and process gently until combined. Add half of the vanilla ice cream and process gently, then add the remaining ice cream and process until well combined.

2 When the mixture is thoroughly blended, add the bananas and process until smooth.

3 Pour the mixture into glasses and serve.

fuzzy peg

ingredients

SERVES 1

2 scoops vanilla ice cream

1 measure lime or lemon juice syrup

cola

ice

method

1 Put the ice cream and lime syrup into a food processor or blender and process for 5–10 seconds with a little cola.

2 Pour into a glass filled with ice and fill with cola.

fig & maple melter

ingredients

SERVES 2

1 1/2 cups hazelnut yogurt

2 tbsp freshly squeezed orange juice

4 tbsp maple syrup

8 large fresh figs, chopped

6 ice cubes, crushed

toasted chopped hazelnuts, to decorate

method

1 Pour the yogurt, orange juice, and maple syrup into a food processor or blender and process gently until combined.

2 Add the figs and ice cubes and process until smooth.

3 Pour the mixture into glasses and scatter over some toasted chopped hazelnuts. Serve at once.

soothing smoothie

ingredients

SERVES 1

1 orange

$^1/_2$ cup cranberries

1 banana

$^1/_2$ cup soy yogurt

fine shreds of orange zest, to decorate

method

1 Peel the orange, leaving some of the white pith.

2 Put the orange and cranberries into a food processor or blender and process. Add the peeled banana and yogurt, then blend until smooth.

3 Pour into a glass, sprinkle with shreds of orange zest, and serve.